Salamander Goo, Poison, and Poo?

Fascinating Salamander Facts

AO PRESS

Written by Jessica Lee Anderson • Photos by Bob Ferguson II

Paperback ISBN: 978-1-964078-44-1

To the Amphibian and Reptile Conservancy for protecting animals and wild spaces. - JLA

To my daughter, Lily . . .Whose curious eyes and brave heart turned rainy nights into quiet acts of kindness. Thank you for every salamander saved, and every moment shared!- BF

All photos taken by Bob Ferguson II unless noted otherwise, including P. 32: Michael Anderson and Phil Dunning. Names of species (current iNaturalist common names) clockwise from top left, unless otherwise noted: Front cover: Marbled Salamander; Interior cover: Large-blotched ensatinas; Copyright: Black-bellied salamander; Dedication: Ringed salamander; P. 4: California newt, Bat cave salamander, Red-spotted newt; P. 5: Red-spotted newts (including eft stages); P. 6: Marbled salamander, Ecuadorian mushroomtongue salamander; P. 7: Coastal giant salamander, Jefferson's salamander, Spotted salamander; P. 8: Pygmy salamander, White-spotted slimy salamander, Seal salamander; P. 9: Red-spotted newt, Fire salamander (photo by Life On White), Yucatan mushroomtongue salamander; P. 10: Blue-spotted salamander, Eastern tiger salamander, Spanish ribbed newt (photo by JAH); P. 11: Big-headed Eryops fossil with a note that this is an extinct amphibian-like animal that is not directly ancestral to salamanders (photo by Jessica Lee Anderson, used with permission: Texas Science & Natural History Museum at The University of Texas at Austin), Eastern hellbender; P. 12: Northern red salamander, Yellow-eyed ensatina, Eastern tiger salamander; P. 13: Cave salamander, Eastern tiger salamander, Yellow-eyed ensatina; P. 14: Spotted salamander, Marbled salamander, and Eastern tiger salamander, Mexican climbing salamander, Pygmy salamander; P. 15: Eastern red-backed salamander, Eastern mud salamander, Yonahlossee Salamander; P. 16: Four-toed salamanders, Long-tailed salamander, Eastern hellbender; P. 17: Two-lined mushroomtongue salamander, Eastern ring-necked snake eating a "lead-phase" Eastern red-backed salamander, Jordan's red-cheeked salamander; P. 18: Northern river salamander, Large blotched ensatina, Imitator salamander; P. 19: Jefferson salamander larvae, Eastern hellbender, Axolotl (photo by Cat'chy Images); P. 20: Arboreal salamander, Two-lined mushroomtongue salamander, Wake's salamander; P: 21: Texas blind salamander (photo by Jessica Lee Anderson), Bat cave salamander, Cave salamander; P. 22: Eastern tiger salamander, Pigeon Mountain salamander, Marbled salamander; P. 23: California newt, Cascade torrent salamander, Blue Ridge two-lined salamander; P. 24: Yellow-eyed ensatina, Arboreal salamander, Northern red salamander; P. 25: Green salamander, Ocoee salamander, North spring salamander; P. 26: Spotted salamanders, Northern red and Northern spring salamander, Spotted salamander and four-toed salamander; P. 27: Blue-spotted salamanders with Atlantic Coast leopard frog, Spotted salamander with wood frog, Eastern hellbender and Wood turtle; P. 28: Eastern red-backed salamander, Four-toed salamander, Northern slimy salamander; P. 29: Eastern tiger salamander research; P. 30: Red-spotted newt, Eastern hellbender, P. 31: Eastern red-backed salamander, Northern red salamander, Smallmouth salamander; Back cover: Northern red salamander

This Book Belongs to:

_____

Differences Between Newts and Salamanders

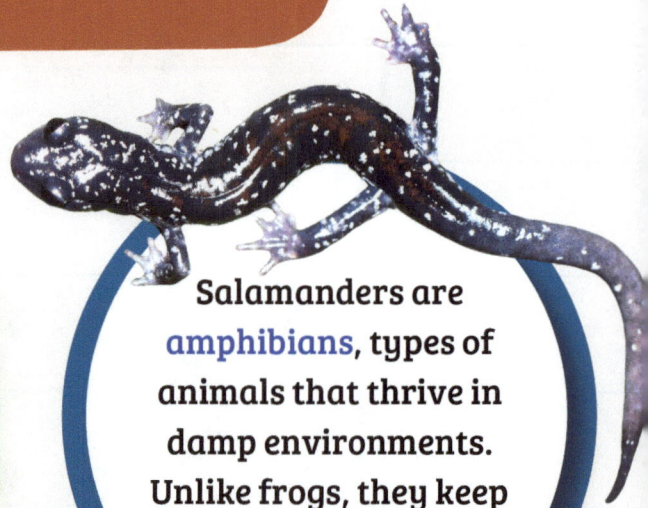

Salamanders are amphibians, types of animals that thrive in damp environments. Unlike frogs, they keep their tails when they become adults.

Newts are a type of salamander that switch between time on land (terrestrial) and in the water (aquatic). Some newt species tend to have rougher, bumpier skin. Not all salamanders are newts.

Eft Stage?

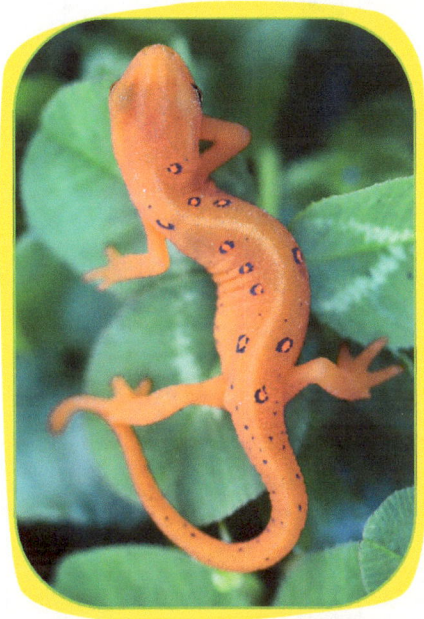

Almost all salamander species lay eggs in the water or on land. After hatching, the newborn babies are called larvae. Some newt species go through an eft stage—they experience changes and move from life in water to live on land. As they mature, they prepare for life back in the water as adults (though some stay efts).

The skin of efts becomes orange or reddish, serving as a warning to predators that they are poisonous.

Sensitive Skin

Salamanders shed their skin as they grow. They'll often eat the shed skin for nutrients.

Even though salamanders have lizard-like tails, they don't have plates or scales. They also lack claws. Amphibians breathe and absorb water through their skin!

Environmental Indicators?

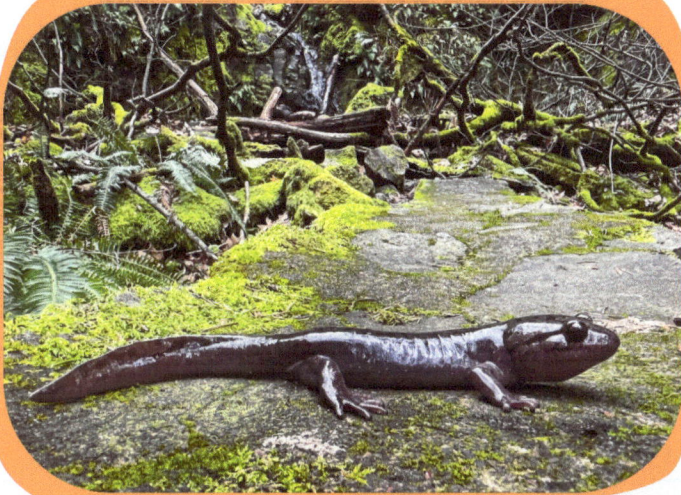

Salamanders are sensitive to changes like pollution or contamination, which is why they're called environmental indicators. Their presence in an ecosystem indicates healthy air and water.

Chemicals and certain types of fungi can pass through salamander skin.

Salamander Goo?

Salamanders have skin glands that produce mucus. This goo prevents a salamander's absorbent skin from drying out. Moist skin helps salamanders breathe and keeps their organs functioning.

Salamander mucus contains protective chemicals that fight fungal and bacterial infections.

Poison!

Salamanders secrete poisonous toxins from their skin glands as a defense mechanism against predators. Poison could cause illness or make salamanders taste disgusting. Salamanders are not a concern for people if they are properly handled or left alone.

Fire salamanders can squirt poison at predators from glands behind their eyes!

Vertebrates

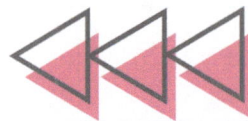

While they may look like they're made of rubber, salamanders are vertebrates, meaning they have a backbone (vertebral column). Their bones are thin and light, perfect for swimming and moving on land.

In case of emergency, Spanish ribbed newts can poke their rib bones through their skin to use as weapons to inject toxins.

"Living Fossils"

Amphibian
Eryops megacephalus
Skeleton (composite)
Permian
Archer County, Texas

Some scientists call the Eastern hellbender and the Japanese and Chinese giant salamanders "living fossils" as their skeletons have remained similar to their ancient relatives that lived before the time of dinosaurs. That doesn't mean the species have stopped adapting, though.

Regrowing Limbs

Scientists are studying how salamanders regenerate lost or damaged body parts to help people with injuries.

If injured, salamanders have an amazing ability to heal. They can regrow limbs, tails, eyes, and other parts of themselves, including their brains!

Terrific Tails

Salamanders have a variety of tail shapes depending on the species, stage of life, and the environment where they live. Their tails store fats and proteins, giving them a boost of energy when they need it.

Certain salamanders wriggle their tails or break them off (autotomy) to escape predators. The tails will grow back in a few weeks, sometimes a different color.

Patterns

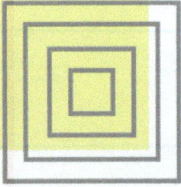

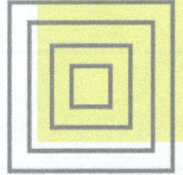

Salamander species can have a variety of skin patterns such as blotches, dots, and stripes. A salamander's patterns are as unique as your fingerprints! Patterns can potentially distract predators.

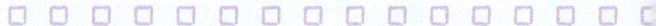

Bright Colors

Bright colors can also distract predators or serve as a warning. Predators eventually learn to avoid prey with bright colors or patterns due to being dangerous or tasting gross. Biologists call warning colorations aposematism.

Camouflage

Many salamanders blend into their environment. Camouflage adaptations help them to survive by going unnoticed by predators. Camouflage also makes it easier for salamanders to sneak up on prey.

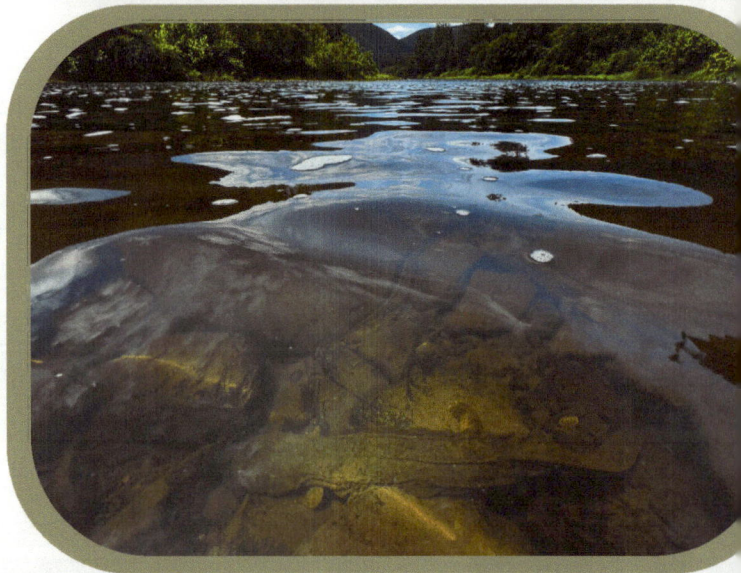

Predators AND Prey!

Salamanders control populations of insects, snails, spiders, and more. Some species actively hunt while others will wait in hiding, ready to use their sticky tongues to catch dinner. Animals like birds and snakes depend on salamanders as a source of food.

Terrestrial

Salamanders that dwell on land (terrestrial) are often found in moist areas, in burrows, and under logs or rocks. Long limbs and flexible necks help them move around. Some species have developed lungs for breathing.

Aquatic

Salamanders that live in water (aquatic) full or part-time often have flat tails. Instead of using sticky tongues, aquatic salamanders open up their jaws to suck food in or to grab a meal. Most aquatic salamanders are born in the water and start life with gills. Many species lose gills as they develop, but a few species never grow out of the larval stage.

Salamander gills are branched and sometimes look feathery. These organs extract oxygen from water, allowing salamanders to breathe underwater.

19

Climbing Salamanders

Some salamanders are adapted to living in the trees (arboreal). Climbing salamanders sometimes have long tails that grip to various surfaces. Pad-like feet help certain salamander species climb. Many salamanders are lungless and breathe only through their skin.

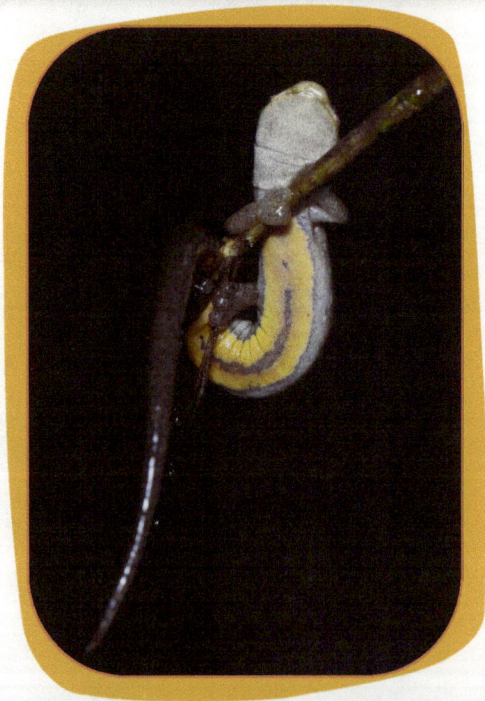

Cave Dwellers

A few salamander species dwell in or around caves, including water-filled caves. Cave-dwelling salamanders can have interesting adaptations like long bodies and tails, less pigment, as well as reduced eyes . . . or no eyes at all.

Survival Strategies

Salamanders are "cold-blooded" (or as some biologists say, poikilothermic). This means they rely on the environment to stay the right temperature. In harsh conditions like winter or during a drought, salamanders slow down to use less energy. Some species may burrow or produce extra mucus.

"Fire Lizards"

The word "salamander" means "fire lizard" in Greek. According to legend, salamanders were thought to be fireproof, especially as they'd crawl out from logs thrown into a fire. Some species survive wildfires by seeking shelter in damp areas or coating their skin with protective foam, but they are not actually fireproof.

Vision and Hearing

Many salamanders have prominent peepers, and certain species appear to have golden or glowing eyes. Their vision is adapted for where they live. They lack outer and inner ear parts, but they can hear ground vibrations. A research study showed certain species can sense sound vibrations through their lungs!

Undulation?

Apart from two-legged sirens, most salamanders have four legs they use to move. Salamanders walk side-to-side with their tail moving them forward. This swaying left and right motion is called undulation.

Salamander legs are usually short and set at right angles to their body.

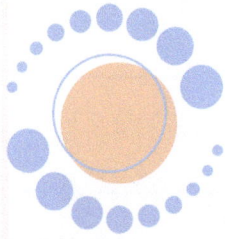

Social Groups

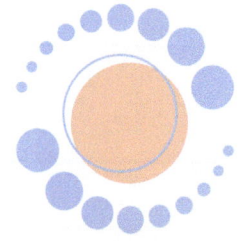

Some salamander species den together in burrows or gather during courtship, though many salamanders prefer to be alone. Salamanders often share the same habitat with other salamander species.

Habitat Overlap

Salamanders share habitats with other amphibians as well as various reptiles!

27

Poo?

Like other kinds of amphibians, salamanders pass waste through a cavity called the cloaca. Certain species mark their space with poop! The scent provides information about identity and territory.

Cloaca

Research

Some researchers study salamanders by injecting elastomers, brightly colored trackers that are soft and flexible. Elastomers don't hurt salamanders. They are a tool to track individual salamanders to learn more about movements, behaviors, growth, and overall health.

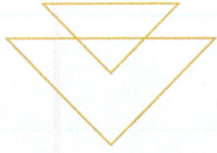

From Mini to Massive

There are more than 700 species of salamanders in the world! They vary in size and weight depending on the species. Some are smaller than a paperclip while others can grow to be about as long as a twin mattress.

Super Salamanders

Salamanders can be found on every continent except Australia and Antarctica.

Scientists are continuing to discover salamander species and learn more about these awesome amphibians! They are also working to save them along with their habitats.

Jessica Lee Anderson is an award-winning author of over 100 books for young readers including the NAOMI NASH chapter book series. Jessica loves spending time in nature and exploring the outdoors with her husband, Michael, and their daughter, Ava! Jessica loves finding salamanders. You can learn more about Jessica by visiting www.jessicaleeanderson.com.

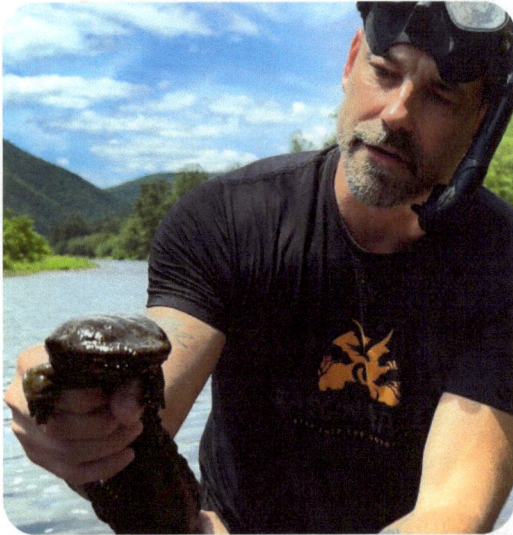

Bob is a naturalist with a compulsion to be outdoors. Wildlife conservation through entertainment, education, fundraising, and fieldwork is his mission and purpose in life. His organization, Fascinature, has donated six figures to saving land in the world's most biodiverse spaces. He even has a frog named after him! You can find him on Instagram @bob_ferguson_fascinature or sign up for his newsletter at fascinature.live.

Check out these other books!

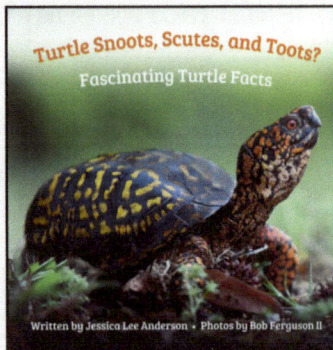

Turtle Snoots, Scutes, and Toots?
Fascinating Turtle Facts

Written by Jessica Lee Anderson • Photos by Bob Ferguson II

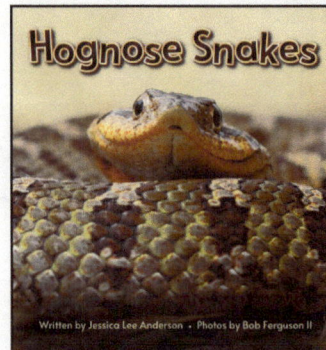

Hognose Snakes

Written by Jessica Lee Anderson • Photos by Bob Ferguson II

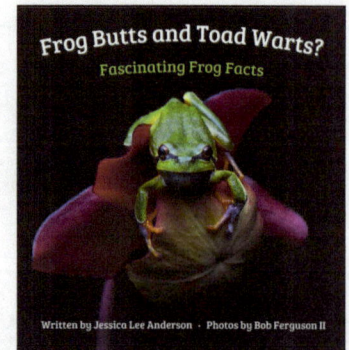

Frog Butts and Toad Warts?
Fascinating Frog Facts

Written by Jessica Lee Anderson • Photos by Bob Ferguson II

www.ingramcontent.com/pod-product-compliance
Lightning Source LLC
Chambersburg PA
CBHW061146030426
42335CB00002B/115